'It's you who are the dogs . . .'

THE CYNIC PHILOSOPHERS

5th century BC–4th century AD

Selection taken from *The Cynic Philosophers: From Diogenes to Julian*

CYNICS IN PENGUIN CLASSICS

The Cynic Philosophers

Anecdotes of the Cynics

Selected and translated by
Robert Dobbin

PENGUIN BOOKS

PENGUIN CLASSICS

UK | USA | Canada | Ireland | Australia
India | New Zealand | South Africa

Penguin Classics is part of the Penguin Random House group of companies whose addresses can be found at global.penguinrandomhouse.com.

This selection first published in Penguin Classics 2016
002

Set in 9.5/13 pt Baskerville 10 Pro
Typeset by Jouve (UK), Milton Keynes
Printed in Great Britain by Clays Ltd, St Ives plc

A CIP catalogue record for this book is available from the British Library

ISBN: 978-0-241-25146-1

www.greenpenguin.co.uk

[LUCIAN], 'THE CYNIC'

This dialogue was probably not composed by Lucian, but is written in imitation of his style and serves as a useful introduction to our subject. The main speaker is supposed to be a typical Cynic; he is identified simply as 'the Cynic' (Kynikos) in fact. Lycinus, the interlocutor, is not otherwise known and is probably invented as well, a mere device to challenge 'the Cynic' to prove the value of his vocation.

LYCINUS: Hey! Who are you with the beard and long hair, but no shirt, no shoes, and practically naked? who prefers a life of wandering more suited to a beast than a human being? who subjects their flesh to pain and hardship, unlike normal people, and who roams from place to place, prepared to sleep on the ground, so that your cloak is covered in filth – not that it was ever soft, fine, or pretty to begin with?

KYNIKOS: Yes, and I don't even need the cloak. But it's the kind that is easiest to get and gives its owner the least trouble to maintain, which is enough for me. I'd like to ask you something, though: don't you think there's something wrong about excessive luxury, and something right about thrift and economy?

L: Of course.

K: Then why, when you see me living more economically than most, do you criticize me instead of other people?

L: Because your life does not impress me as more economical than others', simply as more deficient — as quite empty, in fact, and impoverished. You're no better off than panhandlers who have to beg for their daily bread.

K: The question, then, comes to this: what does it mean to have enough or too little? Shall we discuss it?

L: If you like.

K: The man whose needs are met can be said to have enough, don't you think?

L: I suppose.

K: And the man who has too little is described that way when his means fall short of his needs and don't match his requirements?

L: Yes.

K: Then nothing is missing from my life, because nothing in it fails to satisfy my needs.

L: Explain, please.

K: Consider any of the things that we've come to depend on, such as shelter. We need it for protection, correct?

L: Yes.

K: All right. And clothes, what are they for? Protection too, I suppose?

L: Yes.

K: But what in the world is 'protection' for? Presumably this 'protection' is meant to improve the quality of life?

L: I guess so.

K: Now do my feet look to be in any worse shape than other people's?

L: I can't tell.

K: Maybe this will help you. What are feet for?

L: Walking.

K: And do you think my feet do any worse a job of walking than most people's?

L: Well, probably not.

K: Then if they fill their function as well, it follows that their condition is in no way inferior.

L: I allow it.

K: Then as far as feet go, it seems I am no worse off than your average person.

L: Apparently not.

K: What about the rest of my body? Is it worse than others'? Because if it's worse, that means it's weaker, strength being the measure of a body's fitness. Is it weaker, then?

L: It doesn't seem to be.

K: Then I don't believe my body in general, or my feet in particular, come up short in the 'protection' department. They would be in poor shape if they were, since deficiency of any kind has a bad effect in any circumstance. Again, my body doesn't seem to be any less well nourished for depending on whatever fortune provides.

L: I would agree.

K: And my body is strong, which proves that the food I'm given is healthy; if the food were unhealthy, my body would be in poor health too.

L: True enough.

K: Well, if that's true, then why fault my lifestyle and call it disgusting?

L: For heaven's sake, because nature – which you are always extolling – and the gods have given us the earth and its blessings for everyone to use, and not just use but enjoy. Yet you ignore these advantages – or most of them — and take no more account of them than do beasts. You drink water like beasts, you eat whatever you happen to find, like dogs, and like dogs you sleep just anywhere, as much satisfied as they are with straw for a bed. Add to which your coat is no better than a bum's. But if it turns out that you are the one justified in needing no more, then God was mistaken to supply sheep with wool, make vines capable of producing sweet wine, and create nature in all its wonderful variety, including different kinds of olive oil, honey and the rest, so that we have a choice of food, of drink that is pleasant, soft beds and other furnishings, fine houses and other cunning inventions. For the products of the arts are gifts of the gods too, which it is a pity to renounce as if we were men condemned to prison and dispossessed. It's even more deplorable when someone denies himself these benefits willingly; that is sheer madness.

K: Well, there may be something in what you say. But consider: suppose a rich man in a spirit of warmth and generosity gave a feast and invited many people of different sorts, some healthy, others sick, and put out a large and varied spread. And let's suppose one of the company grabbed and ate all of it, not just the food put before him, but what was at a distance from him and intended for the less fortunate guests — and this though he was in perfectly good health, and having but the one stomach needed little enough to be satisfied but was apt to burst by devouring so much. What would you think of such a person? Would you consider him reasonable?

L: No.

K: Well mannered?

L: No.

K: Now imagine that someone at the same table, ignoring the range of dishes, settled instead on the one closest to him which is sufficient for his needs, and ate it politely without even a glance at the other provisions. Wouldn't you think him better bred and better mannered than the other person?

L: Of course.

K: Well, do you get my point or must I spell it out?

L: Tell me.

K: God is that gracious host who provides many dishes of various kinds, so that his guests can have whatever suits them – the healthy, the sick, the strong and the infirm. We are not supposed to eat all of them indiscriminately; each should take what is set in front of him and of that only as much as he really needs. You resemble the guest who, in his greed and gluttony, helps himself to everything – and not just what's easy of access from local land and water. You import your pleasures from the ends of the earth, always prizing what's exotic over what's regional, what's expensive over what's cheap, what's hard to get over what's near to hand. In short, instead of a simple life you choose to fill it with unnecessary complication. Because all this expensive stuff which is supposedly so conducive to happiness and which you hold so dear costs a lot in terms of pain and aggravation. Just look at gold, which is so sought after, or silver, or expensive houses, fancy clothes, and all that goes with them.

Then consider at what price they're acquired in terms of trouble, pain and danger – or rather in terms of blood, death and shattered lives, not just because many people die at sea searching for these luxury goods or ruin their health manufacturing them, but because they are the source of so much intrigue and conflict among you, setting friend against friend, child against parent, even wife against husband.

And these calamities all occur despite the fact that bright colours do nothing to make clothes warmer, gilded roofs afford no better shelter, drink tastes no more appetizing for being served in gold or silver cups, nor is sleep sweeter when taken in ivory beds. In fact, you will often find that people of status cannot get any rest in their ivory beds, wrapped in their expensive blankets. I need hardly tell you that rich and spicy foods are no more nourishing but can actually harm our bodies and induce disease. Why add the things we do and suffer for the sake of sex? Yet how easy it is to allay this passion, unless we are addicted to perversions. Nor is it enough for us to show ourselves mad and dissolute in the pursuit of sex, nowadays we twist everything from its natural use, like people who would treat a coach not as a coach but a carriage.

L: And who does that?

K: Why, you do – when you order men about like beasts of burden, making them carry you on their shoulders in sedan chairs as if you were travelling by carriage, while you recline in state above, yelling directions down at them as though they were donkeys, 'Not this way, fool, that!' And the more often you indulge in such behaviour the greater the world regards you. What about those who use edible things not just for food but for dyes, like the manufacturers of purple dye – aren't they also making an unnatural use of God's creatures?

L: I cannot agree with you there, the cuttlefish is just as suited to provide dye as food.

K: But that's not what it's for. In the same way you could make a punch bowl serve as a teacup if you had to; but that is not its purpose. In the end, though, no one can give a complete account of the misery such people create for themselves, it's too much. Yet you blame me for wanting no part of it when I live like that well-bred guest whom I described. I enjoy what's easily available, preferring what costs least to get, and don't hanker after delicacies imported from the ends of the earth.

And there's this to consider: if my life reminds you of a beast's because my needs are few and meagre, then by the same argument the gods would be even worse off than animals since they have no needs at all. But to really appreciate what it means to have few wants as opposed to many, consider that children require more than adults, women more than men, the sick more than the healthy – wherever you look, in fact, you'll find that the needs of the inferior amount to more. It follows that the gods stand in need of nothing; and those who most resemble the gods need hardly anything at all.

Take Heracles, the best man that ever lived, practically a god and rightly honoured as one. Do you imagine that it was ill fortune that made him go about dressed in a lionskin, forgoing the things that you consider essential? No, Heracles could hardly be called unfortunate, he saved others from bad fortune, nor could poverty be the cause of his austere habits when he could go anywhere he wanted on land or sea. In all his labours he got the better of everyone, everywhere, and in his time among men he never met his match. Or is it your view that he could not afford shoes or a bed, which is why he travelled so light? No, the idea is absurd; the fact is he had strength and willpower; he chose to control, not indulge, his desires.

Theseus, too, the son of Poseidon, according to legend, the king of Athens, and the best man of his day – didn't he take after Hercules? He chose to go about shoeless and barely clothed too, and let his hair and beard grow out. In this he was like all the men of ancient times. They were better men than you, and not one of them would have shaved any more than a lion would submit to having its mane cut off. Smooth, soft flesh becomes a woman; but as they were men, they chose to look like men. They believed that a beard enhanced a man's appearance like a horse's or a lion's mane, which God gave these animals for no other reason than to enhance their majesty. In the same way God has given men the complement of a beard; and so it's the men of old that I admire and choose to imitate. I disdain the rich food and fancy clothes of the man of today, not to mention the unnatural fashion for smoothing and shaving every part of the body, the private parts not excepted.

My prayer is that my feet be just like hooves, as Chiron's were said to be; that I need bedclothes no more than do lions, expensive food no more than dogs. Let the whole world be bed large enough for me, let me call the universe my home; and may I always prefer the food that's easiest to acquire. May I never need gold or silver; and I wish the same for my friends, since greed for money is the source of society's wars, plots, murders and divisions. And behind it is the unceasing lust for more. So let such desires keep their distance. I hope never to hanker after more than others, but instead be granted the capacity to do with less.

There you have an outline of our ambitions, ambitions,

to be sure, different from those of the masses. And since we differ from them so much in character it isn't surprising that we should differ in appearance. What is surprising, rather, is how you appreciate that actors and musicians should have a characteristic dress and uniform, but don't afford philosophers the same privilege. You believe instead that they should look the way most people do, though most people are hardly worth emulating. But if a philosopher be allowed his own uniform, what better one to have than one that shocks people who have no principles, a uniform that is about the last style of dress they would choose for themselves?

So naturally my appearance tends towards the rough and shaggy, with a worn cloak, long hair and bare feet. Yours, on the other hand, is indistinguishable from that of catamites, with the same colour and softness of coat, having the same large wardrobe, same hair, same shoes, same perfume. Yes, you even smell like them now, the richest among you the most, and yet what, in that case, can people like you really be worth? You are no more capable of work than they are, no less addicted to pleasure. You eat like them, you sleep like them, you walk like them – or, rather, don't walk like them, but prefer to be carried around like baggage on litters or in coaches. My feet take me wherever I have to go. And I can put up with any amount of cold or heat and not complain about the gods and their works because I am poor, whereas you, because of your wealth, are never happy about anything but always dissatisfied. You cannot put up with what you have, but must have whatever is lacking. In winter you want summer, in summer, winter, when it's hot you want cold, when it's cold you want hot – like people who are sick and never content but always complaining. But if in their case their sickness is to blame, in yours it is you who are responsible.

Next, you try to reform us and get us to change because we often are ill-advised in what we do. But you give no thought to your own actions, basing none of them on rational judgement, only on impulse and habit. You are just like people caught in a flood, carried along wherever the current takes them. You go wherever your desires lead. Your situation is like that of the man in the parable who mounted a wild horse who bolted, and with the horse in full career he couldn't dismount. Then they passed someone who asked where in the world they were headed. 'Ask the horse,' the man managed to answer. Now if someone asks you where you're off to, if you're honest you will simply say that your desires will decide – the desires of pleasure, greed and ambition, to be precise. Then it's anger, or some other emotion like fear, that seems to direct you. For you are on the back of not one but many horses, and different ones at different times, but all of them out of control, which is why you end up in ditches or falling off cliffs. And you have no presentiment that any such disaster awaits you.

This worn cloak, however, which you make fun of, my

long hair and this style of dress are so effective that they afford me a life of quiet, doing whatever I like, with whomever I like. No ignorant or uneducated person will come near me because of how I dress, and the fops turn around after spying me a long way off. Men of real refinement and intelligence seek me out, and those who aspire to virtue — the latter especially, since their company affords me the greatest pleasure. I don't hang about the doors of men that society considers happy. Their gold crowns and purple robes are absurdities to me which I can only deride.

I would have you know that my appearance is suited, not just to men of virtue but to the gods, for all the fun you make of it. Examine the statues of the gods and see whether they resemble more you or me. And not just the Greeks', go and inspect images of foreign gods as well and see whether they are depicted in paint or marble with long hair and a beard like me, or close-shaven like you. Most of them, too, you will find are shirtless. So how dare you describe my appearance as shabby when it even suits the gods?

DIOGENES

Diogenes of Sinope established Cynicism as a practical philosophy. Throughout its long history he remained the model by whom all later Cynics defined themselves. Anecdotes of widely varying credibility dominate the tradition about the man, but their cumulative effect in the intellectual history of the movement is reason enough to offer translations of even some of the more dubiously authentic ones.

DL 6. 64

A man once said to him, 'You know nothing, and yet profess to be a philosopher.' 'Aspiring after knowledge,' he said, 'already amounts to practising philosophy.'

DL 6. 60

One day he was asked what he did to deserve the epithet 'the dog'. 'I fawn on people who give me alms, I bark at them if they refuse me, and I snap at scoundrels.'

DL 6. 49

He once begged money from a statue. Asked what he thought he was doing, he answered, 'Getting used to being refused.' When he begged – a practice he began owing to his poverty – he used to say, 'If you've given to others, then give to me too; if you haven't, now's a good a time to start.'

THEMISTIUS, ON VIRTUE, P. 44 SACHAU

The Athenians called Diogenes 'the dog' because he slept in fields, or in front of doorways when he was in town. Diogenes welcomed the name because he found it agreed with his habits. You know how Plato in the *Republic* [375e] describes a dog's instincts: just by sight they learn in time to be on friendly, familiar terms with certain people. The philosopher, however, is endowed with reason, a faculty of discrimination superior to sight. With reason he learns to distinguish between friends and enemies so as to get closer to the former while scaring others off. His aim in getting close to friends is not to bite them or let loose upon them a shower of abuse, but to improve their character by giving them candid advice. As to enemies, even his savage attacks improved their character by exposing their faults to the light.

DL 6. 61

He used to flout convention by eating in full view of everyone, in the heart of Athens' civic centre. People took offence at this once and stood around him, calling him 'dog'. 'It's you who are dogs,' he came back, 'standing around me, watching me eat.'

ANTH. PAL. 16. 333

Satchel, cloak, a barley-cake soaked in water and squeezed tight, a staff to hold before him and lean upon, and a ceramic mug – these are all the accessories essential to a Cynic philosopher's life. Anything else is superfluous. And even one of these turned out to be one too many. For seeing a ploughman taking a drink from his cupped hands, Diogenes addressed his mug, 'Why was I lugging you around with me all this time?'

DL 6. 22–3

According to Theophrastus in his *Megarian Dialogue*, Diogenes discovered the means of dealing with circumstance by observing a mouse running about, with no need of a bed, no fear of the dark, no desire for commonly considered creature comforts. He was the first, some say, to fold his cloak, since he needed to sleep in it too. He carried a pack in which he kept his food. He would use any place for any purpose, whether it be eating, sleeping or conversing. He also used to say that the Athenians had furnished him with living quarters, meaning the Stoa of Zeus and the procession storehouse.

The staff he first began to use for support following an illness. After that, however, it, and the satchel, were his constant accessories when he travelled, although he did without them in town. That is the testimony of Olympiodorus, an Athenian magistrate, of Polyeuctus the orator, and of Lysanius, son of Aeschrio. He wrote to someone to be on the lookout for a place for him to live. When the man was a long time about it, he took up quarters in the cask in the Metroön of Athens, as he tells the story himself in his letters. In summer he would roll around in scorching sand; in winter he embraced marble statues mantled in snow. He practised every kind of self-discipline.

DL 6. 35

He said he modelled himself on conductors of the tragic choruses: they also encourage the choristers to sing a little sharp, with the result that they end up singing right on key.

DL 6. 71

Nothing in life, Diogenes would say, has any chance of success without self-discipline. With it, however, anything was possible. So why not choose to be happy by avoiding vain effort and focusing only on what nature demands, instead of making ourselves miserable with needless exertion? You can even derive pleasure from *despising* pleasure once you get used to it. Then pleasure becomes as distasteful an experience as being deprived of pleasure is for people who have not gained self-discipline. That is what Diogenes said and what he did, defacing the moral currency by consulting nature and ignoring convention. He said his life had the stamp, as it were, of Heracles, since he valued nothing more than freedom.

He sneered at high birth, honours and all such worldly distinctions, calling them camouflage for vice. The only genuine country consisted of the world as a whole. He held that wives should be shared among men, and equated consensual sex with marriage. The sons of such unions were, in turn, sons of the state at large.

He saw nothing wrong in robbing temples. Nor, in his opinion, was it wrong to eat the flesh of any animal. He did not even look upon cannibalism as immoral, citing its practice among foreign nations.

DL 6. 63

Asked where he was from, Diogenes responded, 'I am a citizen of the world.'

When Alexander the Great met and spoke with the great Diogenes in Corinth, so struck and amazed was he was by the man's worth and singular way of life that, in thinking back on their conversation, he would often say, 'If I were not Alexander, I would like to be Diogenes.' By which he meant, 'I would gladly devote myself to a life of reason if I were not already putting philosophy into action'. Notice he did not say, 'If I were not a king I would be Alexander', or 'If I were not rich and an Argead'. He did not prefer good fortune to wisdom, or value royal clothing and a crown above the Cynic cloak and satchel. In saying 'If I were not Alexander I would be Diogenes', he meant to say, 'If it were not my purpose to fuse Greek with barbarian, to traverse and civilize every continent, to explore the limits of land and sea and extend Macedon's borders to the edge of Ocean, to spread and disseminate Greece and its culture through Asia bringing peace and justice to every race, I would not sit idle and wallow in the prerogatives of power. I would instead contend with Diogenes in simplicity. But as it is you must forgive me, Diogenes, if I emulate Heracles, take after Perseus, and follow in the footsteps of Dionysus, the god by whom my royal family was established and from whom it descends. I want to see Greeks again celebrating a victory dance in India, and reviving the Bacchic revels among the wild mountain people beyond the Caucasus. There too we have report of holy men called gymnosophists, devoted to God and likewise inured to an ascetic way of life peculiarly their own.

In frugality they outdo Diogenes since they manage without a rucksack and do not store food but gather and eat whatever the earth produces raw. For drink they have flowing rivers, while leaves and turf serve them for bedding. Through me they will get to know of Diogenes and Diogenes will learn about them. Like Diogenes, I am also under an obligation to deface the coinage, in my case by imprinting Greek civilization on the barbarian.

And now a general assembly of the Greeks was held at Corinth, where a vote was passed to mount an expedition against the Persian empire. Alexander was named commander. Many statesmen and philosophers came and congratulated him. He had hoped to find Diogenes among them since the philosopher happened to be in Corinth at the time. But Diogenes took not the slightest note of him and continued to spend his days in the suburb of Craneum. So Alexander personally called on the man, and found him lounging in the sun. Diogenes stirred a bit when he saw this entourage approach, and turned his gaze in their direction. The prince hailed him, and offered him anything within his power to bestow. 'Get out of the way of the sun,' the other replied. Such pride and nobility, evinced by his evident nonchalance, is said to have made a great impression on Alexander. His attendants just laughed as they wandered off, but for his own part Alexander was heard to say, 'Truthfully, if I were not Alexander, I would choose to be Diogenes.'

DL 6. 58

On one occasion, when he was scolded for eating in public, he said, 'But it was precisely while in public that I grew hungry.' Some people also ascribe this anecdote to him. They say that Plato saw him scraping vegetables. Approaching him, he told him in a confidential tone of voice that he wouldn't have to submit to such work if he would just join Dionysius' entourage. To which Diogenes, likewise under his breath, said that he, Plato, would not have to be part of Dionysius' entourage if he weren't too proud to scrape vegetables.

DL 6. 41

Once he stood some time under a driving rain. Observers took pity on him. But Plato happened by and told them to move on if they really pitied him – an allusion to what he took to be Diogenes' wrong-headed vanity.

DL 6. 40

Plato defined Man as a featherless biped. The definition was generally well received. But Diogenes refuted it by plucking a chicken, bringing it by Plato's Academy, throwing it over the wall while yelling, 'Here's your man for you, Plato!'

DL 6. 41

In the full light of day, a lamp in hand, he used to go about crying, 'I'm on the lookout for a man.'

PHILO, ALL GOOD MEN ARE FREE, 121–3

The Cynic philosopher Diogenes was possessed of such poise and dignity that when he was captured by pirates who barely fed him enough to live, rather than let circumstances get the better of him, or be intimidated by his captors, he challenged them with the following argument. 'It is ridiculous, when pigs and sheep are provided with enough provender to make them sleek and fat before they're taken to market, to reduce the best of animals, man, to nothing but skin and bones by starving us. It only means you'll get less for us than you otherwise would.'

So he was given a sufficient allowance. The day he was to be auctioned off with the other prisoners, he sat and ate in a cheerful mood, not forgetting to share some of his food with the other captives. One of them, however, was overcome to the point where he could not speak for anxiety and grief. Diogenes addressed the man thus: 'Try to stop brooding, and take whatever we get. As Homer says,

Even fair-haired Niobe thought of food again finally,
She whose twelve children were slain in her palace,
Six daughters and six sons still in the flower of youth.'
[*Il.* 24.602–4]

A motivated buyer questioned him as to what he could do. 'I know how to govern men,' he said with perfect frankness – his soul, it seems, giving spontaneous expression to the free, fine and royal element in his nature.

By report he was close to ninety when he died. Accounts differ as to the cause. One has him seized by colic after eating raw octopus. In another version he held his breath until he passed away . . . According to yet another tradition, he sustained a bad bite to his foot when feeding a dog pack with pieces of octopus, a wound that finally carried him off. But Antisthenes in his work *On Philosophers and Their Disciples* reverts to the view that he died of self-suffocation. The story is that he was camping in the Craneum, the exercise area outside Corinth, when his friends arrived as usual one day and found him wrapped in his mantle head to foot. They thought he was sleeping, although it was not like him to nap or doze during the day. Pulling the cloak away, they found his body inert. The consensus was that he had deliberately taken his leave of the world.

Supposedly, though, his followers then fell to arguing over who should have the honour of burying him. It even came to blows. The young men's parents and estate managers had to intervene, until the decision was made to bury the great man by the gate leading to the Isthmus. A pillar was placed on his burial mound, crowned with the likeness of a dog carved from Parian marble. Citizens of Corinth subsequently dedicated bronze statues on the site. On one the following verses were inscribed:

Even this bronze will tarnish with time: but eternity itself cannot
efface your name. For you alone pointed Man towards the path
through life of greatest independence and least trouble or inconvenience.

DL 10. 8, 119

Epicurus branded the Cynics enemies of Greece . . . In the second chapter of his book on *Ways of Life* he says that no enlightened person would choose the Cynic way, or take up begging.

JOANN. CHRYSOST. *IN EPIST. I AD CORINTH. HOMIL.* 35.4

[The apostles performed acts of mercy from pure, selfless motives.] Not so the Greek philosophers. As threats and enemies to our common nature, they acted in a spirit of perversity. [Crates], like any fool or madman, threw all his property into the sea on no good grounds . . . Everything they did they did with a view to being admired. The apostles, in contrast, both accepted what was given them and in turn gave so freely to the poor that they endured a constant state of hunger . . . Consider their laws also, how sensible they were and without a trace of vanity. 'Having food and shelter,' he said [I Tim. 6:8], 'let us therefore be content.' Compare the man of Sinope, Diogenes, who dressed in rags and lived in a barrel on no rational grounds. And while he certainly amazed the masses, no one profited from this arrangement. Paul, in contrast, did not behave likc this since he did not want anyone's admiration. He wore normal, decent clothes, lived in a house like most people, and practised all the virtues without exception. The Dog sneered at such behaviour, lived scandalously and shamed himself in public, driven by a mad passion for notoriety. For if anyone looks into the reason why he chose to live in a barrel, he must conclude that ostentation alone will account for it.

CRATES AND HIPPARCHIA

(fl. 326 BC)

As Diogenes' first pupil, it is not surprising that Crates occasionally displays some of his master's abrasive manners and acerbic wit. But what stands out in the tradition concerning him are deeds of supererogatory good will, especially in restoring peace to warring households. He is the most conspicuous representative of the philanthropic strain in Cynicism. In the account of his relations with Hipparchia we find the same pattern of gruffness, alternating with and finally yielding to warmth and intimacy. Their story is significant not only as highlighting the more benign side of Cynicism but, in Hipparchia's case, demonstrating the school's willingness to extend women the same respect with regard to every value that they recognized that mattered to them.

According to Antisthenes in his book *Successions of Greek Philosophers*, Crates was converted to Cynic philosophy when he witnessed the performance of a tragedy in which King Telephus of Mysia was shown dressed in rags, carrying a satchel. He was moved to sell his property and distribute the sizeable proceeds (he came from a rich family) to his native city of Thebes at large. And so seriously did he commit to philosophy that he is memorialized in verses by the comic poet Philemon, who describes a person who aped his ways: 'In summer he wore a shaggy coat so as to be another Crates, and in winter dressed in rags.' Diodes relates how Diogenes himself induced him to sell his grazing lands, then toss the proceeds into the sea. He also says that he entertained Alexander the Great for a time, much as Hipparchia had welcomed Philip, Alexander's father, into her home. He often had to use his Cynic staff to drive off relatives bent on recalling him to his old, conventional way of life. But he stuck to his purpose. Demetrius of Magnesia says that he gave a sum of money to a banker, asking him to divide it among his children should they adopt a conventional, bourgeois existence. But if they followed him into Cynicism the banker was to donate the money to the city, since as philosophers his children would have no need of it. Eratosthenes has a colourful story to the effect that he had a son by Hipparchia (of whom more later). After the boy, Pasicles, reached adulthood and had completed his military service, Crates escorted him to a house of prostitution. It was here, he said, that he had been introduced to sex himself. Adultery, he said, led to tragedy, death or exile being the usual denouement. Intrigues with prostitutes, on the other hand, were matter for comedy, inducing madness through prodigal spending and merrymaking.

APULEIUS, *FLORIDA* §14

It was Diogenes' words, and others that spontaneously suggested themselves to him, which influenced Crates to at last rush off to the centre of the city and publicly renounce all he owned as so much trash and excess baggage, more hindrance than help. When his actions drew a crowd, he announced in a loud voice, 'Crates hereby grants Crates his freedom.' And from then until the day he died he not only lived alone, but remained scantily clad, free of property – and content.

APULEIUS, *FLORIDA* §22

Crates, the well-known disciple of Diogenes, was honoured at Athens by men of his own day as though he had been a household god. No house was ever closed to him, no head of a househould ever had so great a secret as to consider Crates an awkward intruder. He was always welcome to help settle a quarrel or a lawsuit among relatives. The poets celebrate how, in the past, Hercules by his bravery subdued all the wild monsters and savage men of legend, ridding the world of them. Even so our philosopher proved Hercules' equal in overcoming anger, greed, envy, lust and all the monstrous vices of the human psyche. He rid them of all these sins, purified families and conquered vice.

Like Hercules, too, he went half-naked and carried his own distinctive club; he even came from Thebes, where men say Hercules was born. Even before becoming Crates, as he is now known, he was numbered among the city's leaders, from a prominent family whose house had many slaves and was conspicuous for its large, open court. His lands were rich and his clothing sumptuous. Later, however, he realized that the wealth he had inherited was no safeguard against life's realities, nor was it something on which he could consistently rely, since nothing is certain and everything is subject to change, and all the riches in the world were of no consequence when it came to living honourably.

It is said that Demetrius of Phalerum was exiled to Thebes, living in disgrace and humble circumstances. He was not especially pleased one day to see the philosopher Crates making his way towards him, since he expected he would be treated to a sample of the candour and harsh words Cynics were notorious for. But Crates greeted him politely and consoled him on the subject of exile, saying that there was nothing shameful or trying about it. Instead, it released him from matters inherently hazardous and uncertain. He encouraged him to rely on himself and his own resources of character. Feeling better and more optimistic Demetrius told his friends, 'Now I regret those duties and concerns that kept me from making the acquaintance of a man like that sooner.'

Hipparchia came under the Cynics' spell. She was captivated by Crates' talk and behaviour. The wealth, birth and personal charm of conventional suitors had no appeal for her; Crates was her all in all. She even threatened her parents with suicide if they would not permit her to marry him. At their urging, Crates did everything he could to put the girl off but without success. He finally planted himself in front of her and disrobed. 'Here is your husband,' he said, 'and here is all he owns. So consider carefully, because you cannot be my partner unless you are prepared to adopt my ways.'

The girl made her choice in his favour. Assuming Cynic attire, she went around with him in public, even accompanying him to private dinners. In fact, this is how she came to be present at a party given by one Lysimachus. Theodorus, the notorious atheist, was also present, and she posed the following sophism to him. 'Anything Theodorus is allowed, Hipparchia should be allowed to do also. Now if Theodorus hits himself he commits no crime. Neither does Hipparchia do wrong, then, in hitting Theodorus.' At a loss to refute the argument, Theodorus tried separating her from the source of her brashness, the Cynic double cloak. Hipparchia, however, showed no signs of a woman's alarm or timidity. Later he quoted at her lines from *The Bacchae* of Euripides: 'Is this she who abandoned the web and woman's work?' 'Yes,' Hipparchia promptly came back, 'it is I. But don't suppose for a moment that I regret the time I spend improving my mind instead of squatting by a loom.'

ANTIPATER OF SIDON, *ANTH. PAL.* 7. 413

Instead of the role of a fashionably dressed woman, I, Hipparchia, chose the Cynics' uniquely demanding way of life. I don't care for shawls secured with clasps, high-heeled leather shoes, or fancy fillets to hold my hair in place. Supplied with barley meal, supported by my staff, with my doubled cloak that serves for dress by day, as bedding on the rocky ground at night, I outdo Atalanta of Arcadia, in so far as wisdom outclasses a knack for nimbly negotiating mountain terrain.

BION

Reading Bion, we can see how, as a school of philosophy, Cynicism evolved, or devolved, into the modern, lower-case epithet 'cynical'. What sentiments survive under his name give no hint of a reforming spirit; at times they call to the mind the world-weary epigrams of La Rochefoucauld or the Nietzsche of Human, All Too Human. *But his literary talent and influence show that he was not a pessimist with nothing to contribute but a talent for churlish humour. He is one of the Cynics' most gifted writers, especially in the creation of apposite metaphors, as evidenced in the fragments below and in the examples credited to him by Teles.*

Bion was by birth a citizen of Borysthenes. Who his parents were, and what his circumstances were like before he turned philosopher, he personally described to Antigonus in plain and honest terms. For when Antigonus put to him the line from Homer: 'Who among men are you, and from where? What is your city and who are your parents?' Bion, knowing that the king had already heard unflattering things about him, replied, 'My father was a freedman who wiped his nose on his sleeve — which is to say, he was a dealer in salt fish — and a native of Borysthenes. He was a man of no distinction unless you count the marks on his face, tokens of his master's cruelty. As for my mother, she was exactly the sort of woman you would expect a man like my father to marry: they met in a whorehouse. Then the whole lot of us were sold into slavery when my father engaged in a bit of embezzling. My relative youth and good looks helped me find an owner in the form of an orator, who left me everything when he died.

'I burnt his books, scratched together all I could, came to Athens and took up the study of philosophy. And now you know all about my glorious family background and social circumstances. So it's time Persaeus and Philonides stopped telling stories about me and you judged me for yourself.'

To be frank, Bion was in many respects a shifty

character and wily sophist. He provided the enemies of philosophy with plenty of ammunition. On occasion he could act superior and indulge in arrogant behaviour. But he left behind many memoirs and useful sayings. Being once asked who suffers most from anxiety, he replied, 'Whoever is most ambitious to succeed.' Asked if it was wise to marry, he answered, 'If your wife is ugly you'll be swearing, if she's pretty you'll be sharing.'

He called old age life's harbour from troubles; everyone, after all, takes refuge there. Fame he called the mother of misery; beauty, he said, only benefited others; and money was the glue that held society together. A spendthrift had gone through his entire patrimony, his lands included. 'The earth devoured Amphiaraus,' Bion said to him, 'but you have succeeded in devouring the earth.' In his view, not being able to bear with misfortune was a misfortune in itself.

He often said that it was better to share one's youth and beauty with others than to take pleasure in the charms of someone else, because the latter habit spelled the ruin of not just the body but the soul. He even criticized Socrates, saying that if he was drawn to Alcibiades but abstained from sex with him he was a fool; and if he was not attracted to him then there was nothing remarkable in his restraint.

The journey to Hades, he used to say, was an easy one; men did it with their eyes closed. He criticized Alcibiades because as a boy he drew husbands away from their wives, and as a young man stole wives away from their husbands. When the Athenians were absorbed in the practice of rhetoric, he taught philosophy at Rhodes. To someone who faulted him for this, he replied, 'I have a supply of barley; am I then to try and trade in wheat?'

He would say that a worse punishment for the Danaids in Hades would have been to make their vessels sound instead of full of holes and leaky. To a chatty young man who pestered him for favours, he said, 'I will oblige you but only if you send friends to plead your case so that I won't have to deal with you face to face any more.' Self-satisfaction he called an obstacle to progress. There was a rich man who worried over every penny. 'He does not own a fortune,' he observed, 'his fortune owns him.' Also: 'Misers of this sort watch over their property as if it were their own, but it may as well belong to others for all the good it does them.' And, 'Young men have courage enough, but knowing when to pick one's battles only comes with age.'

He said that good sense surpassed the other virtues as much as sight excels the other senses. And we should not malign old age considering we all hope to reach it. A notorious misanthrope had a particularly black look one day. 'I don't know whether you have met with bad luck,' he said to him, 'or a neighbour with good.' According to him, low birth was inimical to free speech, 'Because it humbles a man, however bold he is by nature.'

Know well the characters of your friends, he urged, to

avoid the reputation of keeping company with lowlifes, or miss the chance to associate with people worthy of your time. When he first turned to philosophy, he studied the doctrines of the Academy, even while attending Crates' lectures. Then he devoted himself to the Cynic discipline, putting on the cloak and satchel; for how better to achieve the ideal of serenity and self-possession? For a time he subscribed to the views of Theodorus the atheist, seduced by the mass of sophistic arguments that filled his lectures. After his Theodorean phase he attended the talks of Theophrastus the Peripatetic.

He had nothing but scorn for music and mathematics. He lived extravagantly, and for this reason he would move from one city to another, sometimes contriving to make a great show. Thus at Rhodes he persuaded the sailors to put on students' garb and follow in his train. And when, attended by them, he made his way into the gymnasium, all eyes soon were on him. It was his custom also to adopt certain young men for the gratification of his appetite and in order to be protected by their goodwill. He was quite the egotist and attached great importance to the maxim that 'friends share everything in common'.

Hence it happened that not a single pupil out of all who attended his lectures became his disciple. And yet there were some who followed his lead in shamelessness. Betion, for instance, one of his intimates, is said to have once addressed Menedemus in these words: 'For my part,

Menedemus, I pass the night with Bion, and don't think I am any the worse for it.' In private conversation he would often promote fiercely atheistic views, the fruits of his association with Theodorus. Afterwards, when he fell ill (so it was said by the people of Chalcis, where he died), he was persuaded to wear an amulet and to repent of his blasphemies against religion. With no one to care for him, his suffering was appalling until Antigonus sent him two attendants. And Favorinus in his *Miscellaneous History* reports that the king himself joined his cortège carried in a litter.

ABBREVIATIONS

Ad Lucil. epist.	*Ad Lucilium epistulae*
Anth. Pal.	*Anthologia Palatina* or *Palatine Anthology*
Arist. Rh.	*Aristotle's Rhetoric*
Benef.	*De beneficiis*
Cic.	Cicero
Codex florent. of John Damasc.	*Codex Florentinus* of St John of Damascus
col.	column
comm. in Epict. enchir.	*In Epicteti enchiridion commentarium*
De off.	*De officiis*
DK	*Die Fragmente der Vorsakratiker*, eds H. Diels and W. Kranz (Berlin 1954), 3 volumes
DL	Diogenes Laertius, *Lives of the Ancient Philosophers*
Gnom. Paris.	*Gnomologium Parisinum*
Gnoml. Vat.	*Gnomologium Vaticanum*
Hercher	R. Hercher, *Epistolographi Graeci* (Paris 1873)
Il.	*Iliad*
In Epist. I ad Corinth. homil.	*In Epistulam primam* ad *Corinthios homilia*
Inst. epit.	*Institutionum epitome*
Joann. Chrysost.	Joannes Chrysostomus
Mem.	*Memorabilia*

Mor.	*Moralia*
Od.	*Odyssey*
Orat. ad Graec.	*Oratio ad Graecos*
Or.	Oration
Pl.	Plato
Plut.	Plutarch
Prov.	*De Providentia*
Sen.	Seneca
Simplic.	Simplicius
Smp.	*Symposium*
Stob.	Stobaeus
Suid.	Suidas or *The Suda*
TD	*The Tusculan Disputations*
Xen.	Xenophon

Square brackets [ ] around a name indicate that the associated work is spurious, that is, probably not written by the accredited author but by someone whose identity is uncertain. Ellipses between square brackets indicate that the passage has been abridged in translation. Text between < > (less than and greater than symbols) indicates that a lacuna has been filled with a phrase or sentence supplied *exempli gratia*.

CHRONOLOGY

BC

469–399	Socrates
c. 445–365	Antisthenes

c. 410–323	Diogenes of Sinope
c. 365–285	Crates of Thebes
c. 350–300	Hipparchia
336–323	Reign of Alexander the Great
c. 334–323	Onesicritus accompanies Alexander on his campaign, about which he subsequently wrote a history.
c. 325–250	Bion of Borysthenes
323	The death of Alexander
c. 235	fl. Teles of Megara
31	Octavian (later Augustus) defeats Cleopatra
AD	
c. 4 BC–65	Seneca the Younger
37–71	fl. Demetrius, the first Cynic of note in the city of Rome
1st–3rd centuries	age of the Second Sophistic
*c.*40–112	Dio Chrysostom, sophist and rhetorician
c. 55–135	Epictetus
c. 70–170	Demonax
c. 125–180	Lucian, sophist and satirist
c. 200	Diogenes Laertius, author of the *Lives of the Ancient Philosophers*, which includes a chapter (6) devoted to the Cynics
331–363	Roman emperor Julian the Apostate
c. 450–500	Sallustius of Emesa, last known Cynic philosopher

1. BOCCACCIO · *Mrs Rosie and the Priest*
2. GERARD MANLEY HOPKINS · *As kingfishers catch fire*
3. *The Saga of Gunnlaug Serpent-tongue*
4. THOMAS DE QUINCEY · *On Murder Considered as One of the Fine Arts*
5. FRIEDRICH NIETZSCHE · *Aphorisms on Love and Hate*
6. JOHN RUSKIN · *Traffic*
7. PU SONGLING · *Wailing Ghosts*
8. JONATHAN SWIFT · *A Modest Proposal*
9. *Three Tang Dynasty Poets*
10. WALT WHITMAN · *On the Beach at Night Alone*
11. KENKO · *A Cup of Sake Beneath the Cherry Trees*
12. BALTASAR GRACIÁN · *How to Use Your Enemies*
13. JOHN KEATS · *The Eve of St Agnes*
14. THOMAS HARDY · *Woman much missed*
15. GUY DE MAUPASSANT · *Femme Fatale*
16. MARCO POLO · *Travels in the Land of Serpents and Pearls*
17. SUETONIUS · *Caligula*
18. APOLLONIUS OF RHODES · *Jason and Medea*
19. ROBERT LOUIS STEVENSON · *Olalla*
20. KARL MARX AND FRIEDRICH ENGELS · *The Communist Manifesto*
21. PETRONIUS · *Trimalchio's Feast*
22. JOHANN PETER HEBEL · *How a Ghastly Story Was Brought to Light by a Common or Garden Butcher's Dog*
23. HANS CHRISTIAN ANDERSEN · *The Tinder Box*
24. RUDYARD KIPLING · *The Gate of the Hundred Sorrows*
25. DANTE · *Circles of Hell*
26. HENRY MAYHEW · *Of Street Piemen*
27. HAFEZ · *The nightingales are drunk*
28. GEOFFREY CHAUCER · *The Wife of Bath*
29. MICHEL DE MONTAIGNE · *How We Weep and Laugh at the Same Thing*
30. THOMAS NASHE · *The Terrors of the Night*
31. EDGAR ALLAN POE · *The Tell-Tale Heart*
32. MARY KINGSLEY · *A Hippo Banquet*
33. JANE AUSTEN · *The Beautifull Cassandra*
34. ANTON CHEKHOV · *Gooseberries*
35. SAMUEL TAYLOR COLERIDGE · *Well, they are gone, and here must I remain*
36. JOHANN WOLFGANG VON GOETHE · *Sketchy, Doubtful, Incomplete Jottings*
37. CHARLES DICKENS · *The Great Winglebury Duel*
38. HERMAN MELVILLE · *The Maldive Shark*
39. ELIZABETH GASKELL · *The Old Nurse's Story*
40. NIKOLAY LESKOV · *The Steel Flea*

41. HONORÉ DE BALZAC · *The Atheist's Mass*
42. CHARLOTTE PERKINS GILMAN · *The Yellow Wall-Paper*
43. C. P. CAVAFY · *Remember, Body . . .*
44. FYODOR DOSTOEVSKY · *The Meek One*
45. GUSTAVE FLAUBERT · *A Simple Heart*
46. NIKOLAI GOGOL · *The Nose*
47. SAMUEL PEPYS · *The Great Fire of London*
48. EDITH WHARTON · *The Reckoning*
49. HENRY JAMES · *The Figure in the Carpet*
50. WILFRED OWEN · *Anthem For Doomed Youth*
51. WOLFGANG AMADEUS MOZART · *My Dearest Father*
52. PLATO · *Socrates' Defence*
53. CHRISTINA ROSSETTI · *Goblin Market*
54. *Sindbad the Sailor*
55. SOPHOCLES · *Antigone*
56. RYŪNOSUKE AKUTAGAWA · *The Life of a Stupid Man*
57. LEO TOLSTOY · *How Much Land Does A Man Need?*
58. GIORGIO VASARI · *Leonardo da Vinci*
59. OSCAR WILDE · *Lord Arthur Savile's Crime*
60. SHEN FU · *The Old Man of the Moon*
61. AESOP · *The Dolphins, the Whales and the Gudgeon*
62. MATSUO BASHŌ · *Lips too Chilled*
63. EMILY BRONTË · *The Night is Darkening Round Me*
64. JOSEPH CONRAD · *To-morrow*
65. RICHARD HAKLUYT · *The Voyage of Sir Francis Drake Around the Whole Globe*
66. KATE CHOPIN · *A Pair of Silk Stockings*
67. CHARLES DARWIN · *It was snowing butterflies*
68. BROTHERS GRIMM · *The Robber Bridegroom*
69. CATULLUS · *I Hate and I Love*
70. HOMER · *Circe and the Cyclops*
71. D. H. LAWRENCE · *Il Duro*
72. KATHERINE MANSFIELD · *Miss Brill*
73. OVID · *The Fall of Icarus*
74. SAPPHO · *Come Close*
75. IVAN TURGENEV · *Kasyan from the Beautiful Lands*
76. VIRGIL · *O Cruel Alexis*
77. H. G. WELLS · *A Slip under the Microscope*
78. HERODOTUS · *The Madness of Cambyses*
79. *Speaking of Siva*
80. *The Dhammapada*

81. JANE AUSTEN · *Lady Susan*
82. JEAN-JACQUES ROSSEAU · *The Body Politic*
83. JEAN DE LA FONTAINE · *The World is Full of Foolish Men*
84. H. G. WELLS · *The Sea Raiders*
85. LIVY · *Hannibal*
86. CHARLES DICKENS · *To Be Read at Dusk*
87. LEO TOLSTOY · *The Death of Ivan Ilyich*
88. MARK TWAIN · *The Stolen White Elephant*
89. WILLIAM BLAKE · *Tyger, Tyger*
90. SHERIDAN LE FANU · *Green Tea*
91. *The Yellow Book*
92. OLAUDAH EQUIANO · *Kidnapped*
93. EDGAR ALLAN POE · *A Modern Detective*
94. *The Suffragettes*
95. MARGERY KEMPE · *How To Be a Medieval Woman*
96. JOSEPH CONRAD · *Typhoon*
97. GIACOMO CASANOVA · *The Nun of Murano*
98. W. B. YEATS · *A terrible beauty is born*
99. THOMAS HARDY · *The Withered Arm*
100. EDWARD LEAR · *Nonsense*
101. ARISTOPHANES · *The Frogs*
102. FRIEDRICH NIETZSCHE · *Why I Am so Clever*
103. RAINER MARIA RILKE · *Letters to a Young Poet*
104. LEONID ANDREYEV · *Seven Hanged*
105. APHRA BEHN · *Oroonoko*
106. LEWIS CARROLL · *O frabjous day!*
107. JOHN GAY · *Trivia: or, the Art of Walking the Streets of London*
108. E. T. A. HOFFMANN · *The Sandman*
109. DANTE · *Love that moves the sun and other stars*
110. ALEXANDER PUSHKIN · *The Queen of Spades*
111. ANTON CHEKHOV · *A Nervous Breakdown*
112. KAKUZO OKAKURA · *The Book of Tea*
113. WILLIAM SHAKESPEARE · *Is this a dagger which I see before me?*
114. EMILY DICKINSON · *My life had stood a loaded gun*
115. LONGUS · *Daphnis and Chloe*
116. MARY SHELLEY · *Matilda*
117. GEORGE ELIOT · *The Lifted Veil*
118. FYODOR DOSTOYEVSKY · *White Nights*
119. OSCAR WILDE · *Only Dull People Are Brilliant at Breakfast*
120. VIRGINIA WOOLF · *Flush*
121. ARTHUR CONAN DOYLE · *Lot No. 249*

122. *The Rule of Benedict*
123. WASHINGTON IRVING · *Rip Van Winkle*
124. *Anecdotes of the Cynics*
125. VICTOR HUGO · *Waterloo*
126. CHARLOTTE BRONTË · *Stancliffe's Hotel*